The
Present Danger

Four Essays on
American Freedom

PAUL G. HOFFMAN

GERALD W. JOHNSON

KENNETH C. ROYALL

HENRY M. WRISTON

FOREWORD BY
STANLEY MARCUS

EDITED BY
ALLEN MAXWELL

Southern Methodist University Press
Dallas | *1953*

FOREWORD

THE TITLE given to this book of essays refers to the battle for men's minds which has been in progress since the end of World War II. This struggle, early christened "the Cold War," has in the past few years generated a heat that has become a serious divisive force in our national life. Most Americans are in agreement about the necessity for preserving freedom, but there the unanimity of opinion ceases. In any state of hysteria there are always two dangers: one, that you will do too much; and the other, that you will do too little. That condition appears to exist in America today, for there are some who, in a sincere effort to preserve our way of life, appear to be willing to cast overboard many of our traditional freedoms. There are others of equal good faith who rely too completely on these same traditional freedoms to preserve them from all dangers.

The freedoms guaranteed to citizens of these United States by our Constitution and Bill of Rights were the result of the experiences of our founding forefathers who had lived under autocracy. They were determined to establish a set of laws that would protect themselves and their posterity against tyranny of the body and of the mind. The Constitution, as written in 1787, did not spell out the liberties of the citizen sufficiently well, so two years later, in 1789, ten amendments were written which have since become known as the Bill of Rights.

These essays by four eminent Americans were delivered as addresses at Southern Methodist University this past spring, in what was called an Institute on American Freedom. The cost of this project was underwritten for the University by a group of twelve Dallas business and professional men, who felt that the times called for a sane re-examination of the origin of our freedoms and their application to the problems of the day. The solutions arrived at independently by these four men are stimulating and encouraging to those who believe that the free life is as worth fighting for today as it was in 1776.

STANLEY MARCUS

Dallas, Texas
[vi] *August 22, 1953*

Contents

American
Freedom
and
Business

PAUL G. HOFFMAN

I DO NOT KNOW of any group for whom the maintenance of freedom has more significance than businessmen. Totalitarian regimes have little or no place for them; in fact, there is no Russian word for a man of business. We in the United States of America are inclined to take freedom for granted. This is not true in other parts of the world. Within the last few weeks I have spent considerable time in Japan, in India, and in Pakistan — countries far removed from us not only in miles, but in development. These countries, almost two centuries after our own struggles for independence and freedom, are now engaged in efforts to establish firmly for themselves government of their people, by their people, and for their people.

In those countries I find that people are intensely excited about two ideological commodities, freedom and liberty. They are excited about them because, to them, these concepts are so new. Much the same sort of excitement, I imagine, was experienced by the citizens of the thirteen American colonies in the days when our Declaration of Independence, our Constitution, and its Bill of Rights were being developed.

Coming back to America and observing some of the phenomena with which we are confronted today, I wonder if we had not best get excited ourselves, forthwith, about our own freedoms and how to maintain them. As businessmen, we dare not restrict ourselves from now on to singing paeans of praise about our free enterprise system. As citizens we dare not restrict ourselves to flag waving and to singing "The Star Spangled Banner." If we want to preserve our free enterprise system we must identify and understand the elements which give that system its strength and then see that those elements are protected and nourished. If we want to preserve our free society we must understand the elements which give it vitality and see that those elements are protected and nourished.

My ideas regarding the elements in our free enterprise system and our free society which should and must be safeguarded are not necessarily definitive — but I do hope that they may stimulate some tough thinking to determine the factors which have made this free enterprise system of

ours and our way of life so outstanding.
The reader who has completed this exercise will, I believe, be in a position to fight for freedom with more effectiveness.

For what it is worth, here is my idea of certain of the underlying sources of strength of our free enterprise system which must be kept undiluted.

First of all, our free enterprise is capitalistic; but our capitalism is unique in that it is a "mutual capitalism." Almost everyone in America has a share in developing it and operating it. From the beginning, only a widely shared capitalism was good enough for America; only a capitalism sparked by *all* the people could do the job.

A second great source of strength of our system is its extraordinary capacity to produce. The whole story of America's amazing productivity can be summed up in this fact: that with about 6 per cent of the world's people, this country produces a third of the world's total goods and almost half of all its manufactured goods.

The key to this productivity is greater output per man hour. And this results from putting ingeniously contrived machines at the disposal of workers — backing up the simple muscle power of those workers with large amounts of horsepower.

I recall one machine tool in our Studebaker plant that cost over a million dollars. With only two men tending it, that machine tool could perform a dozen operations on the cylinder head of an aviation engine — operations that previously required a hundred men working twenty-five machine tools of less efficient design.

The American factory worker fifty years ago had, as a general average, only three-fourths of *one* horsepower behind him. Today he enjoys the help of eight horsepower. On the farms, at the beginning of this century, "horsepower" was literally just that. Now a typical tractor alone gives the farmer the power of forty horses.

The third source of our strength lies in the wide and equitable distribution of the wealth we produce. Generally, when a proposal is made for equitable distribution of wealth, it calls for taking something away from those who have and giving to those who have not. That is one way revolutions start. But in America higher productivity makes it possible to take care of those whose incomes are low

through the equitable distribution of
newly created wealth. That's what has
happened in the United States — we have
made capitalists out of millions of our
fellow-citizens. Peter Drucker made a
cogent observation on this point:

We have learned in these fifty years that productivity is a social principle, and not just a
business principle. In other words, increased
productivity must contribute to greater income of the many, to greater job security of
the workers, to greater satisfaction of the
consumer, to be any good at all. It is not
enough for it to contribute only to profits.

A look at what has been happening to
the pattern of wealth distribution in the
United States may be in order here.

The statistic undoubtedly most familiar
is that there are almost forty million auto-
mobiles for our population of 153,000,-
000. But here are some figures that seem
to me even more significant. In 1949, 26
per cent of all wage earners in the United
States received $3,000 or more in wages
and salaries. But ten years before, in 1939,
only 15 per cent had received an income
of equal purchasing power — an increase
of about 70 per cent in a decade. No de-
pendable figures are available as to the

shift that has taken place between 1900 and 1950. But in each decade an increasing percentage of the total wealth produced has gone to the lower-income group.

Fourth, our free enterprise system is unique in its capacity for change. It rolls with the punches. It has undergone major changes in almost every decade, and it continues to evolve. It remains pioneering, venturesome, and flexible. It never rests on its oars. In other words, it is still unfinished business.

It is this capacity for change, this buoyancy of our American system, which sharply differentiates it from Marxism. That ideology, now called communism, claims to be the wave of the future. It's not. It was out of date when it was introduced in Europe in 1848. Today it is more rigidly reactionary than any right-wing capitalistic economy of which I have knowledge. And our American system, in contrast to it, is truly progressive.

A fifth element of our strength is found in our practice of competition. Maybe no one who has to stand up to stiff competition really likes it, for it is no bed of ease. But we recognize in the freedom to compete for consumers' votes of approval

in the market place a source of vitality, and
and a natural pressure toward the improvement of our standards of living.
Competition not only raises the quality
of our output, but it safeguards the quality of our inner life. That is why we insist
upon *fair* competition — that is, competition according to the rules of the game.

A sixth point of strength in our system
is the fact that decisions are made by
many rather than a few. There is no
other economy on earth that even begins
to compare with ours from that stand-
point. I've noticed in many countries in
Europe and Asia which are leaning toward socialism, or carrying on with an
outmoded form of capitalism, that deci-
sion-making becomes the prerogative of
a tight little monopoly. I also find that
where only a few are making decisions,
only a few are capable of making them.
So such a society loses a part of its
strength by letting wither away the wills
and abilities of the many to make decisions and take risks.

A seventh point, one of the most re-
markable of all the features of our free
enterprise system, is the important place
occupied by voluntary groups. People
from other countries often poke fun at

and
Business

[9]

us because we are joiners. It is true that we are the greatest joiners in all the world. But it is this fact that has made ours the strongest society in all the world. We organize on a voluntary basis to improve our villages, our schools, our industries, and our local and national economies. As businessmen we learned long ago to join forces, to improve conditions not only for all businessmen, but for our communities and for the nation. We have learned how to co-operate in order to have a bigger and better market in which to compete.

THESE SEVEN POINTS by no means comprise the full roster of those elements that make our enterprise system unique and productive. Our system would wither and die if it were not for the contributions made by modern merchandising — by selling and advertising. We can't have the advantages of large-scale production unless we have large-scale merchandising activities. But that is a subject all by itself.

Those of us who are businessmen should especially take to heart the basic fact that our free enterprise system can exist only in a free society. It could not exist in

Russia or in Poland. It cannot exist in any
society where individual freedoms are denied, or abrogated. So to keep our system, and keep it productive and successful, we must keep our society free.

Men cannot fulfil their capacities as individuals unless they are free to think, free to inquire, and free to speak their minds.

It is said that none of us can have freedom to think unless each of us accords to all others the same right. We cannot have freedom to inquire unless academic freedom is maintained. We shall not have freedom to speak our minds — unless the safeguards of the Constitution and the Bill of Rights are generally understood and respected.

We must be on guard against any and every activity which puts in jeopardy our rights as individuals to determine for ourselves what we should think, what we should discuss, and, with proper regard for the rights of others, what we should do. Freedom of thought is a basic human right, from which flow freedom of religion, freedom of the press, and freedom of assembly and association. But freedom of thought is a sterile and meaningless right, unless we are free to discuss, to criticize, and to debate. Criticism, discussion, and debate are the only means of peaceful progress. All history shows that without them a society must stagnate and die.

The thought control of dictatorships is imposed by force, but discussion, criticism, and debate can be stifled by fear as well as by force. Persecution by public opinion can be as powerful as purges and pogroms. Schoolteachers, government clerks and officials, and even businessmen can be frightened out of their rights under the First Amendment as effectively as if that amendment were repealed. Frightened men are, at best, irresponsible in their actions and, at worst, dangerous. Of all the forms of tyranny over the mind of man, none is more terrible than fear — to be afraid of being oneself among one's neighbors.

Of late, some of our people — often good people — have been blindly arousing just this kind of fear. In their zeal to combat communism, they have been betrayed into using methods and measures which impair the sources of our strength and thus play directly into the hands of the Kremlin. They are making criticism socially dangerous. They try to force conformity through fear.

As a result, too many of our fellow-citizens have been afraid to speak out. In far too many cases, decisions — often decisions in high places — have been influenced by fear. And this in a nation which has grown to greatness and glory because it has recognized the rights of nonconformists and dissenters!

If we want to assert the free nature of man and strengthen our free society, we must insist that with due regard for the laws of libel and slander, the right to criticize must be maintained. This right is meaningless unless it extends to the thoughts with which we disagree. I, for example, disagree most intensely with the *Daily Worker's* tagging of every anti-Communist as a Fascist. I also disagree intensely with those who make reckless charges of communist sympathies. But I would not for a moment suppress these irresponsible critics. They must not be suppressed. They must be answered.

ANOTHER DEEP SOURCE of strength in our free society is justice. A free society, to endure, must be a just society. Everyone concerned about freedom in America must be concerned about justice, too. One reason why we must encourage criticism is that we must encourage people to point out such injustices as yet remain in America, and to fight for their elimination. An unjust society cannot long endure. An injustice against one person puts all in danger. Only by safeguarding the rights of minorities do we safeguard the rights of majorities. Racial and religious discrimination, special privilege, and inequality of opportunity for growth are on the wane in this country; but, where they still exist, these and other injustices must be discovered and rooted out.

These convictions of mine are at best merely guidelines to a program of action. The forming of that program must be a task for our best minds — the minds of great stature.

The situation I have described is one that has engaged the attention of the Ford Foundation. Recently the trustees of the Foundation were so concerned over this situation that they set up the Fund for the Republic. The members of this Fund's board of directors are a distinguished group of Americans. They propose by every means possible to help promote an understanding by all our people of the need for protecting the sources of our

strength. That's work in which all of us

will have to engage for decades to come. *and*

Business

It is not a work that can be handed to specialists and accomplished merely through research and the circulation of materials. No work that seeks to go to the heart of our free society to espouse the cause of the individual person can be the exclusive concern of any national body. It must be the concern of individuals in their own neighborhoods and villages everywhere.

We *are* faced with real dangers. There *is* a conspiracy directed from Moscow to infiltrate free societies with disruptive agents and fellow-travelers. It *is* the declared purpose of the enemies of freedom to use freedom in a calculated strategy to sap the strength of free peoples, to divide and confuse.

We have to study these tactics and take counsel together in our local groups on how to frustrate the success of such tactics without undermining the foundations of our own faith. That calls for understanding on two fronts: what our freedoms mean, and what the nature of the threat to them is.

Without such a public awareness there is little basis for trust and confidence. We risk becoming victims of unreasoning fear

— fear of the unknown. In the very act of trying to safeguard our institutions we may blindly contribute to the disruptive tactics which we fear more than we understand.

Nothing, in my judgment, can be more important in these tense times than to renew our faith in freedom through the widest possible study and discussion of the meaning of our way of life. Instead of withdrawing from our voluntary associations in fear and suspicion, we should at this time gather together and reason together about the most fundamental concern we have — the sources of our strength.

If we dedicate ourselves anew to making in America a demonstration of a free, just, and unafraid society at work, we can show all the world that a government of the people and by the people can do more for the people than any other kind of government on earth.

American
Freedom
and
the Press

GERALD W. JOHNSON

THE RELATION of American freedom and the press is singular. The word is precisely applicable, for this relation is unique, curious, and somewhat enigmatic, all of which are elements of singularity. It is unique because it has not been established in any other great nation. It is curious because it was established here informally, not to say inadvertently. It is enigmatic because it has defied exact definition for more than two hundred years.

The First Amendment to the Constitution provides that "Congress shall make no law . . . abridging the freedom of speech, or of the press." We carelessly refer to this prohibition as establishing freedom of the press, but it does nothing of the sort; it refers to a pre-existing freedom, antedating the government established by the Constitution and explicitly exempted from its control. Linked with freedom of worship, speech, and assembly, it was regarded by the framers of the Bill of Rights as a component of that general liberty which the Declaration of Independence lists among the three inalienable rights with which men are endowed

[19]

by their Creator, as opposed to special liberties won from government through
some sort of grant.

The concept of liberty as a right which
freemen had from God, before there was
a king, is certainly not distinctively
American. It is far older than the United
States. It dates back at least to Runny-
mede, and Acton takes it to Palestine.
"When Christ said, 'Render unto Caesar
the things that are Caesar's and unto God
the things that are God's,'" declares the
British historian, "those words marked
the repudiation of absolutism and the inauguration of freedom." There could be
no more absolute claim of the divine
origin of liberty.

Yet recently Henry Steele Commager,
an American historian, pointed out in an
article in the *New York Times* that no
other nation has included freedom of the
press in that liberty which derives from
a source higher than the king. On the
contrary, it has been carefully excluded;
even in Great Britain such liberty as has
been accorded the press has been in the
nature of a grant from king or parlia-
ment. Even the document that is fre-
quently described as the Great Charter
of a free press, Milton's *Areopagitica*, is

a plea for abolition of the licensing of
books as a measure of practical statesman-
ship, rather than as the assertion of a right
antedating government, and inalienable.

Freedom of the press was incorporated
in the inalienable American rights in 1735,
when Andrew Hamilton, a Philadelphia
lawyer, put it there on his own responsibility. Hamilton was defending John
Peter Zenger, a printer in New York, who
had been haled into court on charges of
criminal libel. Since Zenger had no defense in law, his counsel took refuge in
morals, and carried the jury with him.

Zenger had published a series of articles
exposing the colonial governor of New
York as a grafter who had not only
stuffed his own pockets but had appointed
to office as gaudy a set of scoundrels as
had disgraced any administration.

This was criminal libel under the law
as it stood then — and as it continued to
stand in England until 1792, when Fox
brought in his famous bill granting freedom of criticism to the English press. The
only question for the jury was, did Zenger publish the articles? Truth was not a
defense, because the purpose of the law
was to maintain not justice but public
order. To insure the stability of govern-

ment lawmakers had felt that magistrates must be protected from criticism tending to bring them into contempt. The more truthful the criticism, the more contemptible the magistrates would appear; hence the legal maxim, "The greater the truth, the greater the libel."

Historically, this position was perfect. Historically, rulers of every type had realized that, as far as their power was concerned, no other danger was to be compared with the danger of public tumult. The ruler might be as bad as Caligula, or as good as Marcus Aurelius, but in either case he knew that his rule and usually his life depended upon maintaining a reasonable degree of order in his realm; and one way of maintaining order was to set up the fiction of the omniscience and benevolence of the government. If magistrates were to be exposed as rogues, this fiction could not be imposed upon the people; hence magistrates must not be exposed.

This was the law when Hamilton undertook the defense of Zenger — not merely the British statute law, but, in substance, the law of all civilized countries. Zenger had published the articles. Of that there was no doubt. Therefore under the law Zenger had no defense, so his counsel sought a defense above the law.

He relied on a principle that has since been repudiated by American courts — the *jus naturae*, the law that has existed from the beginning of the world, and which it is the duty of legislatures to find. "The Common Law is not a brooding omnipresence in the sky," said Justice Holmes in 1916, "but the articulate voice of some sovereign or quasi-sovereign that can be identified." But in 1735 the Common Law, as men conceived it, *was* something like a brooding omnipresence in the sky. Statutes were not supposed to be creations of lawmakers, but efforts to express in words the law that existed independently of legislatures; it followed that a legislature of limited understanding, or one inaccurately informed, would misinterpret this brooding omnipresence and so write bad law that no human authority could make good.

In the case of Zenger, Hamilton argued that a statute forbidding a man to tell the truth was in conflict with the *jus naturae*, and therefore could not be good law, regardless of the authority of kings, parliaments, and precedents. The jury agreed, and found Zenger not guilty.

The verdict was so widely popular that the royal governor dared not set it aside. So Zenger's became a leading case and something very much stronger — one of the articles of our political faith. Fifty years later, when the Constitution-makers were at work, the principle that freedom of the press is an alienable right was so generally accepted that the body of the Constitution does not mention it at all, and the Bill of Rights is concerned only to make sure that some heretical later government could not undertake to abridge it.

But the informality with which this principle was introduced into our system has given infinite trouble to jurisconsults and writers on politics ever since. The *jus naturae* has gone into the discard along with the social contract; but finding a substitute for it has been difficult. "The voice of some sovereign or quasi-sovereign," said Holmes; but the only voice identifiable in this case is the voice of Andrew Hamilton who, far from being either a sovereign or a quasi-sovereign, was a stubborn and contumacious fellow, who would be described today as a subversive character, and probably would be deported.

Hamilton, from Philadelphia, was called into the Zenger case in New York because the governor's party had disbarred Zenger's original counsel and threatened to disbar any other lawyer who took the case. That was just the kind of thing to appeal to Hamilton, who hated all parties. He was a born maverick, although an astonishingly able one. He practiced law brilliantly enough to win the Zenger case. He practiced architecture brilliantly enough to design Independence Hall in Philadelphia. He practiced business brilliantly enough to make two or three fortunes. But first, last, and always he practiced independence. If he had been living in 1952 it is easy to believe that he would have denounced both Eisenhower and Stevenson and, although a leading corporation lawyer, he would have died rather than tell a Congressional investigating committee that he was not a Communist.

This was the character primarily responsible for the peculiar relation of American freedom and the press. He was in the most rigorous sense of the word a free man — free from thraldom to any

human master, and over and above that,
free from the prejudices, prudences, and
conventions that hold most of us shackled
and gyved mentally and morally, if not
physically. Needless to say, he was also
a bold man; for no man is really free
unless he is bold to the point of reck-
lessness.

NATURALLY, a doctrine enunciated by a
free spirit has given trouble to later generations not endowed with the contempt
of danger that inspired this man. We are
reluctant to admit that we owe our liberties to men of a type that today we hate
and fear — unruly men, disturbers of the
peace, men who resent and denounce what
Whitman called "the insolence of elected
persons" — in a word, free men. It re-
minds us of the extent to which we have
become prisoners of our doubts and fears,
and we do not like such reminders. For
freedom is always purchased at a great
price, and even those who are willing to
pay it have to admit that the price is
great.

Thomas Jefferson, for example, asserted that if he had to choose between
government without newspapers — and
he meant a free press — or newspapers

without government, he would unhesitatingly choose the latter. Yet the same Jefferson, tormented by biting and unjust criticism during his presidency, could write:

It is a melancholy truth that a suppression of the press could not more completely deprive the nation of its benefits, than is done by its abandoned prostitution to falsehood. Nothing can now be believed which is seen in a newspaper. Truth itself becomes suspicious by being put into that polluted vehicle.

When he wrote that, in 1807, Jefferson was contending with what Adlai Stevenson called a "one-party press" of a virulence surpassing the worst we have seen in our times. He was not complaining of a free press, but of a licentious press; for freedom to do what one knows is wrong is not liberty, it is license. Toleration of license is a heavy price to pay for freedom, but Thomas Jefferson was willing to pay it, since he knew no other way to obtain it. As in the biblical parable of the tares in the wheat, there is no way of ripping out the weeds in the field of journalism without bringing the grain with them.

Alexander Hamilton, in the *Federalist,*

Number 84, stated the relation between
American freedom and the press in ex-
plaining why no guarantee of a free press
appears in the body of the Constitution:

Who can give it any definition which does
not leave the utmost latitude for evasion? I
hold it to be impracticable, and from this I
infer that its security, whatever fine declara-
tions may be inserted in any constitution re-
specting it, must altogether depend on public
opinion and on the general spirit of the people
and of the government.

Later, the First Amendment was added
in deference to widespread demand, but
the amendment actually restates Hamilton's assertion. It forbids Congress to
abridge the undefined freedom of the
press; but a later amendment in the same
Bill of Rights asserts that all powers not
enumerated or prohibited in the Constitution are reserved to the states or the
people; and as every state has embodied
in its own constitution something like the
First Amendment, this power is reserved
to the people. They may abridge freedom
of the press at will; and never doubt that
they do so.

All writers on this subject from Alexander Hamilton down to Walter Lipp-

mann and Zechariah Chafee have had to

admit that freedom of the press has no
independent existence, but is merely one facet of freedom of the people. It is a common assertion that suppression of a free press is the first act of every modern dictator, but the assertion is inaccurate. Gagging the press is merely a reflection of the first act of a dictator, which is to abolish the freedom of the people, with or without their consent.

So it is a dubious assertion when one calls freedom of the press the bulwark of our liberty. It is closer to truth to say that freedom of the press is the measure of our liberty. If "the general spirit of the people" is low, nothing can save freedom of the press; but when that spirit is high, no politician can lay hands upon it.

At the same time, it would be fatuous to deny that here is a case of action and reaction; a high-spirited people creates a free press, but it is incontestably true that a free press tends to keep them a high-spirited people. Any evidence, therefore, that freedom of the press is being abridged is just cause for alarm both for what it reveals and for what it portends about freedom in general.

From John Milton to Morris Ernst nobody except newspapermen has ever claimed that the craft of journalism is entitled to a special position for its own sake. Freedom of the press does not mean freedom of the printer except as his freedom is essential to the freedom of the reader. It is my right to read whatever I choose to read that makes it necessary to set the printer free to print anything. Obscenity and libel are banned because I have no right to read them, and with my right to read, the printer's right to print them vanishes.

BUT NO FREEDOM EXISTS without a corresponding responsibility. Because I am free to read anything, it becomes my duty to read the truth; and by the same token, it becomes the duty of the newspapers to print it.

Here is the acid test of both the press and the public. Lippmann long ago pointed out that a well-established newspaper can afford to defy its advertisers, because it controls a product, publicity, that they are bound to have. It can defy politicians and win fame and fortune by doing so. It can even defy what Hamilton called "the rich and well-born" yet continue to flourish. The one element it cannot defy is the average reader, for if it loses its readers it has lost everything.

Yet every newspaperman of experience knows that there are times when to print the exact truth, and all of it, would be disastrous to circulation. The American public is not without its Sacred Cows, and to touch them is perilous in the extreme. We recognize this in act, if we are reluctant to admit it in theory. Last spring a pair of country weeklies in North Carolina received the most distinguished award in American journalism, the Pulitzer prize for public service; they earned it by attacking and destroying a vicious organization that nevertheless was popular with large numbers of people in their area. And it was well earned, for it took courage to assail the Ku Klux Klan in Columbus County, North Carolina, although it would be safe enough to do so in New York.

If an American newspaperman had nothing to fear but the law, he would be in a much happier position, for he knows, or can find out, what the law is. But what the prejudices of his readers are he learns only by crashing into one; and a single experience of that kind fills him with a dread of prejudice that he never felt for the police, uniformed or secret.

I do not see how any rational human being could suspect Arthur Hays Sulzberger, publisher of the *New York Times*, of being a radical; but in a public address last January Mr. Sulzberger made the statement that in his opinion communism is not the only or necessarily the most dangerous threat to American liberty. He saw the possibility that excessive fear of communism may effect a lowering of "the general spirit of the people" that would be more disastrous than all the spying, and lying, and cursing that the Communists have done or can do.

If Mr. Sulzberger is right— and he offered impressive evidence in support of his opinion — then the alarm should spread through press and public alike, and each should engage in soul-searching. For they react on each other, and since liberty is indivisible they will rise or fall together.

The press cannot escape some responsibility if freedom of the press is abridged. I do not have in mind its more obvious sins — the sensationalism of one of its segments, its pandering to depraved tastes, its inexcusable invasions of privacy, and its willingness to make a fast buck at any expense to truth, justice, and honor. We do have newspapers like that, and they ought to be destroyed; but unfortunately it cannot be done, for their destruction would do more damage than they do. They are at worst nuisances, rather than grave threats to the spirit of the people.

I have in mind reputable newspapers, owned and managed by men who feel that the craft offers rewards not found in the pay envelope or in the dividend rate. The fellows who turn out the lurid rags are mere day laborers, who if they were paid as well, would just as cheerfully work as scavengers or on a pick-and-shovel gang. But there are craftsmen who remain in newspaper work because they find a satisfaction in it that they could obtain from no other employment; and it is these that I have in mind; for they, being respected, really do influence the general spirit of the people.

That these constitute a free press is as doubtful as that Americans in general constitute a free people. True, American newspapermen have no Goebbels standing over them with a knout. But there are dictatorships that are not political, yet effective. One of them is that fear by which all Americans are hag-ridden. We are not a free people because, to a very large extent, Malenkov dictates what we shall do and especially what we shall not do. He does it by contraries, but he does it. Whatever Malenkov approves, that we must despise; whatever Malenkov hates, to that we must adhere. He has bound us, not with his Red army, but with the chains of our own fear; but he has bound us.

The question for the American press is, to what extent has it contributed to the generation of this fear? To answer, "Not at all," would be fatuous. For twenty years the press — and I mean the highly respectable press—has been propagating fear.

Part of it was inevitable. The press was compelled to report the rise of the Soviet power and its malignant hatred of free institutions, for these are facts, and to have ignored them or glossed them over would have been nothing short of criminal. Although our real troubles with Soviet Russia began in 1945, long before that the most reputable section of the American press had been consistently and persistently sounding alarms, asserting in the teeth of all the evidence that the very foundations of American liberty were crumbling and that the American way of life was on the verge of extinction.

The excuse for this is that we were passing, along with the rest of the world, through a revolutionary period. With us it did not produce, as it did in other countries, riots, bloodshed, subversion of the constitution, and civil war, but it affected us profoundly.

I NEED NOT LABOR the point when one small item can tell the whole story. In 1929, according to Professor Arthur F. Burns, who is described today as President Eisenhower's chief economic adviser, the richest 5 per cent of our population received 34 per cent of the total disposable individual income; but in 1946 the same 5 per cent received only 15 per cent of the national total. True, they had lost nothing, since 15 per cent of the 1946 income was worth as much as 34 per cent of the 1929 income. But the point is that in seventeen years we moved rather more than half way toward complete equality of income, which is certainly revolutionary.

This was news, big news, the biggest news of our generation, and the press did not fail to report it. But the story had

two important angles. One was that we
were moving with revolutionary speed.
The other was that we were moving in a
smooth and orderly fashion while other
nations, all over the world, moving in the
same direction at comparable speeds, were
blowing to pieces.

I submit that the news value of the
second angle was the greater. The fact
that we were moving in the same direction as all other civilized nations was interesting, but not sensational. What else
would you expect? But the fact that while
many others were breaking under the
strain, the fabric of our government held
together sturdily was not what everybody
expected, was, indeed, precisely what most
of the outside world did not expect.
Above all, it was what the Communists
least expected, and it knocked the foundation from under their dialectical ma-
terialism.

Throughout those fateful twenty years,
with constitutions exploding like fire-
crackers all around us, we made just two
changes in our organic law — we repealed
prohibition and we changed the date of
the inauguration. Repeal was actually
counterrevolutionary, that is, it was a re-
turn to the original system, while the

Lame Duck amendment was purely a matter of convenience having no bearing on basic freedom. All the necessities of the new era we met by changes in the statutes. In other words, the American system successfully rode out the storm that wrecked half the nations of the world.

This should have bred a mood of confidence in our institutions that would have enabled us to meet any possible threat with calm. But when the Soviets began to show their teeth in 1946 and 1947 we were anything but serenely assured. On the contrary, we were so shaken that we fell promptly into a hysteria that has gravely endangered every honest man.

For this the press was partly responsible because it lost its sense of news value. Through all those years it played up the fact that we were moving, and played down the fact that we were moving smoothly. It emphasized the commonplace and neglected the extraordinary. It spread all over the front page the story "Dog Bites Man," and relegated to page 17 the story "Man Bites Dog." So it convinced many Americans that instead of being astonishingly strong, we were half ruined; naturally, then, when the

Bear made a pass at us, these already ter-
rified Americans went into spasms that
drove many to advocate throwing overboard the whole Bill of Rights.

Of course the press was not entirely
responsible. Partisan malice, economic
greed, and racial fanaticism all played
their parts. But this descent into bad
journalism should engage our particular
attention.

The reasons for it are many and some
of them are obscure, but I am satisfied
that they do not include, except in scat-
tered instances, any real "treason of the
clerks." I think it was done in all sincer-
ity, through lack of understanding, not
through lack of fidelity.

There is, of course, no mystery at all
as regards the group of journals that may
be included under the generic term of the
scavenger press. They were motivated by
the only thing that ever moves them,
to wit, money; they will cheerfully sell
the truth, or even tell the truth, provided
they get their thirty pieces of silver.

But such rags are common nuisances
rather than serious threats to liberty. I
refer to reputable newspapers that, being
respectable, do influence "the general
spirit of the people." And these, I sub-

mit, have propagated fear when the facts justified confidence.

One thing that blinded them was, no doubt, that human reluctance to take the next step that afflicts us all.

Another and more powerful factor was the explosion of war, which engenders hatred. A hater is never a free man, because he is the slave of his passion.

Another was the widespread revolt against intelligence, which has been stimulated by the prostitution of physical science to the ends of destruction. Thirty years ago science, to the layman, was the broad avenue to life and healing; today it is the descent to Avernus, the road to destruction and death. No wonder its professors have sunk in the esteem of men.

But the dominant factor, I am persuaded, is economic. A modern metropolitan newspaper is Big Business. Only a great millionaire, or a millionaire corporation, can own a large-city newspaper now; and in all the world there is nothing more timorous than a million dollars, except ten millions. In revolutionary times the rich are always the people who are most afraid, and the press is rich.

For emphasis, I repeat that I see no calculated treason in this. I am unable to

[39]

discover a personal devil anywhere. Every factor I have mentioned is beyond the control of any individual, and some are beyond human control.

But while we may not have power to deliver ourselves from peril, I do believe that we have some degree of control over our reaction to threats. Many a badly scared man has gone ahead and done his duty anyhow, and that is what constitutes valor. The United States is in danger; it has been in danger every day of its existence; and it will remain in danger as long as it remains a free nation. But its moments of greatness have been the moments when it took counsel of something other than its fears; and I cannot see this present as such a moment.

Yet the need for greatness continues and grows more urgent. In 1787 Alexander Hamilton, then urging ratification of the Constitution, wrote:

It seems to have been reserved to the people of this country, by their conduct and example, to decide the important question, whether societies of men are really capable or not of establishing good government from reflection and choice, or whether they are forever destined to depend for their political constitutions on accident and force.

Hear how that is echoed by Vera Dean,
in a book published this year:

With a record of freedom untarnished by fear-inspired restrictions, the United States can look forward to playing effectively its newly-acquired role of world leadership. But let that record be placed in doubt, and this country will appear to other nations as just another great power using its armaments not for the defense of human liberties but for selfish interests of its own.

The people, by their conduct and example, will decide. The people, that is to say, you and me — not Mr. Eisenhower in the White House, not Mr. Sulzberger in the office of the *New York Times*, not the joint chiefs of the Pentagon; that is, not politics, nor the press, nor physical power; but you and me. For we create the general spirit of the people, and as that goes up or down, so do all our freedoms rise and fall.

American
Freedom
and
the Law

KENNETH C. ROYALL

AมERICA'S GREATEST MENACE today is the combined communism and totalitarianism of Russia and its satellites. Their prime objective is to destroy throughout the world our type of democracy and freedom. We must, to the limit of our ability, oppose these hostile forces as effectively as possible — oppose them at home as well as abroad.

Frankly, I would place absolutely no limit on doing anything — and I mean anything — which is necessary to protect us from these communist forces; provided, however, that such protective conduct would not in itself endanger our nation.

As has been often said, the real test of our American system of justice is not whether we treat fairly those with whom we agree, but whether we treat fairly those with whom we do not agree. Are we meeting this test today?

In my native Wayne County in North Carolina about thirty years ago, a Negro from Philadelphia, together with some local friends, attempted to rob and actually did murder a country grocer.

Feeling ran high, and in short order a white mob moved on the courthouse intending to abduct and lynch the Negroes.

Some younger members of the bar and a few other members of the American Legion quickly got together to defend the courthouse. There ensued what is known locally as the Battle of Wayne Courthouse. Though the building itself suffered considerably from gunfire of many kinds, the outnumbered defenders fought off the attack and seriously wounded the leader of the mob.

Some days thereafter the accused Negro was tried — with a National Guard company this time protecting the square from another growing mob. Upon a confession and other clear evidence the defendant was promptly convicted and later executed — despite the best efforts of counsel appointed by the court.

An interesting sequel came a few months later. The leader of the mob had lost his leg in the courthouse battle. Despite this fact, he was tried and promptly convicted of inciting to riot, and was sentenced to the state penitentiary — the sentence being rendered in the same courthouse he had attacked.

This episode left several indelible impressions on my mind: first, the impassioned, cruel, bloodthirsty, and inhuman faces of the lynch mob, a mob bent on death beyond the law to a fellow human being — death to him largely because he was a member, though an unworthy one, of a minority and then overawed race.

On the other side of the picture I still envision the determination of that small group of good citizens who successfully fought off the mob — and who thereafter, despite the tumult around them, calmly and legally and successfully proceeded to punish the lynch leader.

But in weighing the whole occurrence then — and in weighing it now — one cannot avoid the conclusion that even if the guilt of the defendant had been doubtful, and if in addition the good citizens of the community had been slightly less firm and courageous, then the mob spirit among some members of a normally decent and God-fearing community would doubtless have unjustly taken the life of a human being. Or — worse still — a jury might well have been swayed or intimidated by the passion of a mob and might have unjustly doomed an innocent man to death.

Other incidents of this kind have unfortunately happened in America under the same or some other type of passion or prejudice or bigotry or intolerance. They may involve matters of life and death, as in the case of the Battle of Wayne Courthouse, or they may involve unjust imprisonment or loss of property — or they may in whole or in part concern an individual's right freely to follow his chosen vocation or to earn a decent livelihood.

Such bias-based mass interference with American justice is not confined to matters of race and color. Some of us remember the Al Smith campaign of 1928 when anti-Catholicism ran rampant through our South. Right now I can see in that election men and women, theretofore known for their judgment and fairness, walking like medieval zealots to the polls with anti-Smith ballots clenched in their hands and with lights in their eyes frighteningly similar to those of the mob in Wayne County.

The Smith campaign was not merely political. It spread human hatred and division among friends and neighbors — and at least temporarily it created a dif-

ficult court situation in cases involving
Catholics. Another type of bias is anti-
Semitism, which is not unknown in court,
although I remember no extreme cases.
And in some of our larger population
areas it is at least rumored that Protestant
minorities may receive less justice than do
others.

However and wherever these situations
arise, they must be met — not by decla-
mations on the Constitution and Bill of
Rights but by determined insistence of
patriotic citizens that our freedom and
fairness before the law be preserved.

TODAY A THREAT involving our system of
justice has arisen in connection with another class of people; our enemies and
potential enemies and alleged friends of
these enemies. This situation, of course,
is not historically new. In fact, it has
arisen before in comparatively recent
years.

Early in World War II eight German
saboteurs landed on our coast; in the
spring of 1942 they were apprehended.
President Roosevelt, by Proclamation and
Order of July 2, 1942, ordered that they
be tried not by a normal civil court, but
by a Military Commission appointed by

the President. Furthermore — and this is
an important point — the President directed that, except with Executive approval, the accused "shall not be privi-
leged . . . to have any . . . remedy or proceeding sought on their behalf, in the
courts."

Counsel which had been appointed for
the accused sought the removal of the direction against the use of the civil courts,
writing the President that "It is our opinion that [the accused] should have an
opportunity to institute an appropriate
proceeding to test the constitutionality
and validity of your Proclamation and of
the Order."

The President declined to make the
change, whereupon counsel for accused
wrote him again:

Our duty requires us to institute (or to have
instituted) . . . at the appropriate time the
proceedings necessary to determine the constitutionality and validity of the Proclamation
and Order. . . . Unless ordered otherwise, we
will act accordingly.

Hearing nothing from the President,
the counsel did "act accordingly." After
the Military Commission case was com-

pleted, they applied to the Supreme Court
of the United States to review the validity
of the commission and its action.

In an unprecedented move the Supreme
Court called a special midsummer session
and heard the cases at length. The evidence before the commission, including
confessions from all of the accused, had
been convincing; the commission had imposed death sentences upon six of the
accused and prison sentences upon the
others. The Supreme Court did not re-
verse this action, nor did it deny the validity of the commission itself.

However, the feature of this court
hearing which is especially relevant is that,
notwithstanding the prohibition of the
President against action by civil courts,
our highest court — and, earlier, a courageous district court — did review and
consider at length the objections raised
to the action by the Military Commission.

This Supreme Court review of enemies'
cases in the midst of a bitter war has been
hailed as a great demonstration of American justice, as has the completeness of the
sharply contested trial before the Military Commission. This view was corrobo-
rated by an unusual action of the accused.

At the completion of the long Military Commission trial, when six of the accused almost necessarily realized that they would be condemned to death, they wrote a joint note to their counsel, which I quote in part:

> Being charged with serious offenses in war time we have been given a fair trial. . . .
> Counsel...has represented our case as American officers unbiased, better than we could expect and probably risking the indignation of public opinion. We thank our defense counsel.

There is some basis for satisfaction at the fulness of the legal procedure that was followed, but there were, too, some less gratifying facts. When the accused were first arrested, there was widespread demand that they be shot summarily. One of our best and most widely circulated weekly magazines even printed a picture of a squad of members of one American Legion post, who offered to do the shooting.

It was after this demonstration of lynch-mob feeling that the Chief Executive of our nation made his attempt to bar any use of the civil courts on behalf of the accused. When, thereafter, attor-

lake shore and burn, by God." The school-
books of Chicago were examined and only
one history textbook of a satisfactorily
patriotic nature was found among those
scrutinized for evidences of un-Americanism. It was asserted that "they showed
definitely seeds of the Rhodes scholarship,
the Carnegie Foundation and the English-
Speaking Union." The superintendent of
schools was suspended, later dismissed.

IN THE 1930's there was a fresh outbreak
against "radicalism," largely stimulated
this time by private agencies. Elizabeth
Dilling published *The Red Network: A
"Who's Who" and Handbook of Radicalism for Patriots*. By the most charitable
standards it was an incompetent work.
Communists, Socialists, radicals, liberals
— in short, anyone left of center — were
tossed into one basket. The book denounced on successive pages Mahatma
Gandhi and Glenn Frank, then president
of the University of Wisconsin; it attacked Albert Einstein and the great
social worker, Jane Addams. The tattoo of
charges against Bishop G. Bromley Ox-
nam was initiated at that time. To cap it
all, about 1,300 persons were listed, "who
are or have been members of Communist,

Anarchist, Socialist, I.W.W. or Pacifist-controlled organizations, and who, . . . knowingly or unknowingly, have contributed in some measure to one or more phases of the Red movement in the United States." This list included such persons as Senator Borah, Mrs. Roosevelt, William C. Bullitt, John R. Commons, Max Eastman, Clifton R. Fadiman, Waldo Frank, Zona Gale — a mélange of people of many shades of opinion lumped into one group.

While the outcry at this time was principally the work of private agencies, restrictive legislation was adopted in several states. Teachers' oaths were enacted in Indiana, Montana, North Dakota, Washington, Michigan, New York, Arizona, Georgia, Massachusetts, New Jersey, Texas, and Vermont. In the town in which I then lived a school committee-man demanded that the school library be purged of all books written by persons mentioned in *The Red Network*. Subsequently Elizabeth Dilling was herself twice indicted for conspiracy and prosecuted in the federal courts. But she had done her share of damage first. By what authority did she and other volunteer censors of American thought presume to

establish standards of political and economic orthodoxy? Who gave them the
power to speak ex cathedra and decide
what was safe to believe and permissible
for free men to utter? Yet they assumed
— and sometimes exercised — the right
to purge our schools. They have successors who arrogate to themselves the same
false authority today.

This episode is instructive. Like all
similar "investigations," it treated communism and socialism, left-wingism, New
Dealism, and even liberalism as one. In
order to avoid admission of this confusion, the phrase usually employed has
been "un-American." "Un-American"
can mean whatever the investigator, public or private, does not like. "Orthodoxy"
is whatever the current sleuth wants it
to be; all else tends to be "subversive."
For example, in 1926 Fred R. Marvin,
editor-in-chief of the *New York Com-
mercial*, said, "Internationalism is the direct opposite of nationalism, it is Socialism, or as often called today Communism." Seldom is the grab-bag quality of
presumed "un-Americanism" put as explicitly as that, but it is implicit in the
publications and statements of most of
the vigilante groups then and since.

During the thirties, as Hitler rose to power, the League of Nations faltered, and appeasement dominated British policy, students became much concerned about peace. Russian "peace" propaganda of the kind with which we are all by now thoroughly familiar put a taint on the very word "peace." Anyone who spoke for peace was accused of being a "Red." In 1933 the Oxford Union voted that it would "in no circumstances fight for its King and country"; that declaration was taken with great seriousness as reflecting a decline in the patriotism of students and in their commitment to patriotic causes. Suspicion about students' loyalty did not subside. In 1940 one of the great metropolitan dailies of this country asked me to tell why college students "seem to hold to a belief that no ideal is worth fighting for." I replied that, when the need arose, students would fight as they always had before; and, indeed, they did.

The most recent phase of the hue and cry is centered in Congress. It was launched in May, 1938, when the House of Representatives adopted a resolution by Martin Dies which set up the Committee on Un-American Activities. The committee explained its own tactics: "While

Congress does not have power to deny to citizens the right to believe in, teach, or advocate communism, fascism, and nazism, it does have the right to focus the spotlight of publicity upon their activities." A later report was even more explicit: "The purpose of this committee is the task of protecting our constitutional democracy by . . . pitiless publicity."

The First Amendment provides that "Congress shall make no law . . . abridging the freedom of speech." The Dies Committee sought to curb unwanted expressions of opinion through the employment of means not contemplated when the Constitution was written. The Constitution contains no warranty that congressmen will be polite, fair, or even intelligent; it does not guarantee that they will not bully people out of their freedom of speech, if people are ready to be bullied.

The Un-American Activities Committee has continually disregarded the warning of Chief Justice Hughes, who, conceding the right to curb *abuse* of free speech, declared:

The rights themselves must not be curtailed. The greater the importance of safeguarding the community from incitements to the overthrow of our institutions by force and vio-

lence, the more imperative is the need to preserve inviolate the constitutional rights of free
speech, free press and free assembly in order
to maintain the opportunity for free political
discussion, to the end that government may
be responsive to the will of the people and
that changes, if desired, may be obtained by
peaceful means. Therein lies the security of
the Republic, the very foundation of constitutional government.

This passage was quoted on May 2, 1953,
by Judge Youngdahl in dismissing the
principal count and three subsidiary
counts in the indictment of Owen Latti-
more. He was re-emphasizing the fact
that there is no available acid test of political orthodoxy.

Since the Dies Committee began to
function, both the use and the abuse of
publicity by Congressional committees
have indeed been "pitiless." Throughout
the last dozen years the Committee on
Un-American Activities has constantly
contributed to the growth of mass emo-
tion by statements and charges — some
justified, but others exaggerated beyond
the bounds of truth. The judicial depart-
ment of the government can offer no pro-
tection against this technique; for, as the
great constitutional lawyer, John Lord

O'Brian, has said, "The increasing use of publicity by legislative committees to intimidate witnesses and others and to hinder and discourage expression of unpopular views has been held to be beyond the reach of the courts."

The misbehavior of some of those who conduct the investigations does not destroy their legality. The authority to make inquiries rests upon the provision in the Constitution that all legislative powers shall be vested in the Congress. At the time of the Teapot Dome episode the Supreme Court made it clear that Congress has sweeping power in this matter. The authority of its committees is clear, therefore, even when their manners are atrocious. The possession of power, however, does not justify its abuse; the greater the power, the greater the need for self-restraint in its use. The key to the success of democracy is the juncture of responsibility with power; this is what committees of Congress need to learn.

One of the most extraordinary aspects of the recent situation is the disparity in treatment of former Communists by the investigators. If a person leaves the Communist party with enough fanfare, he is treated with utmost respect, indeed almost canonized. People like Louis Budenz, Elizabeth Bentley, and Whittaker Chambers are recalled again and again for fresh "revelations"; everything they say is accepted as gospel truth, even though lying was habitual with them until they recanted communism. Others who also joined the party, but took no active part and committed no subversive act (as these people admittedly did), and later quietly left it, are pilloried for having once been passive members.

This inequality of treatment becomes the more striking because the professional former Communists who testify so freely spread fear, hate, and divisiveness. Indeed, they do it to a degree which must be pleasing to still-active Communists, one of whose characteristic objectives is this very thing. In fact, if these recanters had only pretended to leave the party and were actually counterspies (as I certainly do *not* assert), they could hardly perform the function of creating confusion more effectively than they have done.

NONE OF THE ABOVE is meant to minimize the very real danger posed by the present world-wide conspiracy, directed from the Kremlin, which is designed to overthrow our form of government, the structure of our economy, and our social order. No one can read the report of the Royal Commission of inquiry in Canada in the Gouzenko investigation without gaining an appreciation of both the reality and the subtlety of the Communist menace, and also the difficulty of coping with it.

Moreover, there were attempts by Communists in the thirties, the forties — and probably the fifties — at infiltration of the American educational system. Evidence is overwhelming that the Communists did attempt to infiltrate labor unions, churches, entertainment, social work, charities, the government, and the armed forces; to assume that they overlooked education would be naïve.

How successful were these attempts? We have three sorts of evidence. First, the behavior of students in the war and after: on this point the evidence is overwhelming — they have behaved admirably. There were no draft riots, virtually no disturbance at all in the mobilization of the largest percentage of the population ever undertaken. Fears expressed over a decade proved utterly groundless.

The second evidence is the behavior of

alumni. Regarding them the evidence is equally overwhelming. America's population includes many who have graduated from schools and colleges during that thirty years. They are the ones Attorney-General Palmer and his successors have repeatedly said had been inoculated with the communist virus. Among that presumably "infected generation" are all the present Congressional viewers-with-alarm. No evidence has been offered that the alumni of the last thirty years are markedly different in their social, economic, and political views from earlier generations. In fact, their politics has recently taken a turn toward more conservative lines.

It has been estimated that at the present time the Communist party has fewer than 30,000 members in the entire United States. That number is much smaller than the 1920 estimates. The real problem before the public, therefore, is not so much the indoctrination of youth with "Red" propaganda; the problem is the recovery of Congressional confidence in the institutions of America. Taming headline hunters would do more toward that end than any other single action.

The third evidence regarding the in-

effectiveness of communist infiltration is
to be found in the disclosures of the various committees which have been investigating subversive activities for years.
Their revelations are of slender substance
indeed. Names are occasionally headlined; then large generalizations are made.
No committee has ever tabulated the
number of Communists or pro-Commu-
nists who have been uncovered in the
schools and colleges; if infiltration over a
period of thirty years had gone very far,
one would certainly expect impressive
statistical results. Instead, every indica-
tion is that the numbers are so trivial that
no one seeking political gain from such
investigations wants to be very specific.

WHY WERE SOME — a few — teachers,
like people in other professions and walks
of life, influenced by communist promises and principles? Without condoning
their folly, we should attempt to understand how some honest people came, for
a time, to believe in communism — or at
least in some aspects of it.

At the close of the first World War
Russia's new government was not recognized by the United States and other leading nations; it was treated as a pariah.

Later, several factors softened the censorious mood of many people. Among these factors was a whole series of Russian reforms. A massive effort against illiteracy was launched — a movement bound to win applause in the United States, which has led the world in universal free public education. Discrimination against races and nationalities within Russia was "abolished." The cultural autonomy of its many peoples was respected. Everyone had a job. We now know that some reforms were ephemeral, others were shallow, and still others existed only as propaganda, without a firm root in reality. Nevertheless nondiscrimination, full employment, land reform, universal literacy, all held a powerful appeal to American sympathies.

The most influential factor in arousing a favorable response to communism, however, was the depression of the thirties, which afflicted the whole world but the United States most acutely and for the longest time. It led many to lose faith in our economy. The "mature economy" idea, later exposed as a gross fallacy, was then accepted and expounded by President Roosevelt himself at a time when his influence and authority were overwhelming.

Politicians were not alone in doubting the resiliency of our economy. Businessmen joined enthusiastically in the NRA, which was designed not by college "theorists" but by practical politicians and hard-headed businessmen so little aware of the fundamental presuppositions of free enterprise that they were ready to abandon their birthright; it was one of the most violent assaults in modern times upon the free enterprise system. Even those who had the greatest stake in traditional economic doctrines quickly turned to the "new" idea. Seeking to meet a desperate situation, they threw economic sanity to the winds. Only a Supreme Court pilloried by the President for thinking in terms of the "horse and buggy" age saved us from utter folly.

As faith in our economy waned, doubt was engendered regarding the virility of the political institutions which formed its framework. In that mood and in those circumstances many felt that democracy had lost its dynamism. To such the available choice seemed to be between the "new" forms of government. Some people, weary of democracy, felt that the

fascist idea was an authentic "wave of
the future." To others fascism seemed to
offer the most immediate, the most direct,
and the most powerful threat to the
United States. Statements by high government officials gave support to that
idea. Nevertheless, Hitler's threat to the
world went virtually unchallenged by the
victors of the first World War. Their
response to aggression was appeasement.
Many who recognized the menacing character of the fascist and nazi governments
believed the Soviet to be the only implac-
able foe of those ideologies. Overconcen-
tration upon the nazi menace blinded
them to the serious dangers that lay within
communism.

Moreover, there were signs that Russia
might try to live at peace with the free
world. In 1933 President Roosevelt re-
versed our policy regarding the Soviet,
granted recognition, exchanged ambassa-
dors, and rather pooh-poohed earlier fears.
The next year Russia entered the League
of Nations, dramatizing the possibilities
of peaceful coexistence, if not collabora-
tion. Then the Communists co-operated
in "popular front" governments.

When war came, we were allied with
Russia. Official censorship concealed from

the American people the failure of the
Russians to co-operate wholeheartedly.
There were warm comments by the President of the United States. It is said that
the Senate arose and applauded as one man
the heroism at Stalingrad; sentimentalism
surrounded the Russians with a rosy hue.

Those were the conditions, of varying
force, at various times, and with various
people, which led some to look upon
communism with a degree of favor. A
few joined the party; others associated
themselves more or less actively with organizations in which Communists had a
hand — sometimes a controlling hand.

Those who espoused such views were
quite wrong in their estimate of the situation. However, they were no more
deeply in error than people who believed that fascism was the authentic
"wave of the future"; they were no more
wrong than those who felt the American
economy was senescent or even fatally ill.

In short, many made gross errors in
estimating the situation. When one adds
together all whose judgment proved
faulty, the total is very impressive.
Among the worst estimators were members of Congress: only four months before Pearl Harbor the draft was extended

by the margin of a single vote. Most of those in error have long since abandoned their error. Yet today only one group among all those who misinterpreted the facts is treated as though it were not only wrong but deliberately disloyal. Were those representatives and senators who voted against the draft intentionally trying to sabotage the defense of their country? No one claims this; yet others whose error was no greater are pilloried.

In this group were some scholars and members of faculties who made emotional, intellectual, and spiritual commitments to communism or participated in "front" activities. My personal opinion based on long observation is that the number was trivial in proportion to the whole; Senator Jenner on April 11, 1953, asserted that the number of communist teachers was "small." And the few communist teachers were seldom in the "sensitive" subjects — the political and economic disciplines. Politically naïve scientists were the most conspicuous victims; and clearly their political views did not relate to their teaching.

THE SUCCESSIVE WAVES of inquiry have reflected the investigators' doubt regard-

ing the integrity of all American institutions — not just educational institutions.
They manifest disbelief in the viability
of our basic social, economic, and political idea. The core of our national ideology
is faith in freedom. In every case these
inquiries stemmed from fear that freedom
and security are incompatible — and the
inquisitors invariably set security above
liberty.

The earliest hysteria was over pro-Ger-
mans during the first World War. The
study of German was dropped from many
schools—as though ignorance were a cure
for anything! Men who taught German
were dismissed from teaching appointments on the flimsiest pretexts; Harvard
helped halt that trend with an act of
courage and sanity when it refused to
barter its integrity for a large sum of
money. Victory put an end to this phase
of doubt of America's intellectual and
moral solvency.

The next surge of hysteria, which opens
the modern phase, was deliberately contrived by a politically ambitious attorney-
general who hoped to become President.
He abused the investigative powers of the
Federal Bureau of Investigation; he in-
cited voluntary spy-hunting; he violated

the law and trampled the Constitution. Mr. Palmer's fortunate departure from office, and the action of a stern and caustic federal judge, ended that inglorious spasm.

Meanwhile the infection had spread to the states, and private groups of viewers-with-alarm were in full cry. New York had the Lusk Committee investigations; the committee's report was in four fat volumes which mentioned membership of teachers in "revolutionary organizations" and said that "in different parts of the State of New York systematic campaigns have been conducted to reach school-children and teach them to detest their own country and government." Real evidence to support the sweeping indictment was slender.

States passed laws requiring teachers' oaths, but the experience of many years has now proved the futility of such legislation. If it had been an effective approach, the uproar would have ended long since; its uselessness is fully demonstrated by the continuing lack of confidence that there has been any improvement as a result of such laws. The recent California episode shows the folly of an approach via an oath. No Communists were identi-

fied or dismissed. Instead, one of our
greatest universities was torn with con-
troversy, disrupted in its vital tasks, de-
prived of the services of distinguished
scholars, and made suspect as a home for
new scholars. It would be hard to imagine
a more futile — or more disastrous —
proceeding if we have any interest in
advancing educational practice and pro-
viding our children with better skills and
attitudes.

The private groups of political vigi-
lantes have changed personnel over the
years, and the root motivation has varied
from time to time and group to group as
new organizations emerged. Some have
been fascist in inspiration and positively
vicious. Some have grown out of a lack
of basic faith in democracy; indeed there
have been occasional explicit denuncia-
tions of democracy as "un-American."
Others have contained sincere patriots
scared to death by a world which had run
beyond their comprehension; they yearned
for "older and simpler" times which never
existed save in their unhistorical minds.
Some would give up the long battle for
freedom in exchange for order and discipline of the masses — which means
tyranny. Nearly all these amateur rooters-

out of "subversion" have this in common
— they have been and are scandalously
incompetent; they spread fear; they impair the functioning of the American
system and tend to disorganize education.

Congressional committees are the most
recent entrants in the confusion sweep-
stakes and are most in the public eye.
Their tactics are often summarized by
the word "McCarthyism." It is a poor
word; Senator McCarthy is a Johnny-
come-lately in hating Communists, having been at it only a few years. It would be
better to call it "Palmerism," in memory
of the man who launched the panic a generation ago. Painful as it may be to attempt to be fair to a man who seems never
to make a like effort, the fact is that Senator McCarthy is neither the first nor even
the worst of the Congressional sleuths.
Both doubtful distinctions belong to the
House. The first was Texas' own Martin
Dies, who developed the technique of
reckless headlines under the guise of "pitiless publicity." The worst also belongs to
the House of Representatives; it was an
explicit, incompetent, and wholly vicious
attempt by the Un-American Activities
Committee, under the chairmanship of
Representative Wood of Georgia, to purge

schools, colleges, and universities of "dangerous" books.

The episode was brilliantly informative
of the wrong way to "purify" education.
The committee so far overreached itself
that it was almost instantly apparent
there was political dynamite rather than
political profit in its shocking behavior.
Its categorical imperative was followed
by a spate of weasel words. It beat a hasty
retreat and tried to pretend that it had
not intended to interfere. Any witness
before a Congressional committee who
made such a series of contradictory asser-
tions as were made by spokesmen for the
committee would be indicted for perjury.

Congressional committees have gone
far beyond the abuse of witnesses. On the
initiative of the Un-American Activities
Committee, Congress attached to an ap-
propriations bill a rider which had the
character of a bill of attainder. The Supreme Court unanimously declared it un-
constitutional; there is no reason to believe
its authors did not know that it violated
the Constitution when they conceived the
trick.

The first time Congress defined communism as subversive was in the Smith
Act of 1940. If teaching had really been

in the parlous condition that a succession of investigations had headlined, some action would have been taken before that time. And if the act had been an effective reply to subversion, investigations need not have continued. Yet the Smith Act only gave them renewed life.

The present investigations of education are directed by Senator Jenner and Representative Velde. Both have been relatively orderly and relatively mild. Perhaps we should be grateful for such crumbs of comfort. But the inquiries are still futile; their net effect is to keep the public needlessly alarmed, to spread fear within and without educational institutions; they sap confidence in the cornerstone of the American system — educational opportunity for all in the highest possible degree.

They exhibit lack of faith in the American family, the American church, and the manifold agencies of enlightenment — since the investigators appear to believe that a few Communists infiltrated in a few institutions can overcome all those stabilizing influences. Common sense should make it clear that if a few obscure teachers are stronger than all our American institutions, the fabric of our

society is weak indeed. That is what is
essentially vicious about these investigations. They all stem from lack of faith
in the strength of the American system.

A full generation of Red-hunting has
led to executive trespass upon the Constitution, to legislative abuse of investigative powers, to the promotion of ruthless
private vigilante groups. Besides the harm
all this has done education, there is a
substantial body of evidence that it has
harmed the government itself and im-
paired the principles embodied in the Bill
of Rights. It is time to stop such subversive activities.

The present federal administration is
headed by a former university president.
He held that post long enough to see this
problem from the inside as well as from
the outside. In bidding farewell to Columbia he said:

When I was asked to come to Columbia by
the trustees, I, like all others outside of university halls, had heard of this constant rumor
and black suspicion that our universities were
cut and honeycombed with subversion and
there was communism lurking behind every
brick on the campus and every blade of grass.
. . . I have found universities in general engaged in how to bring up, how to teach, how
to develop fine citizens to serve in a free de-

mocracy. . . . This is not to say that there may
not be people among us false to the doctrines
and the basic principles in which we believe.
If they are there, if they are sworn enemies
of our system, if they believe in its destruction by force, then I know of no one who
will be more anxious than the true teacher to
get rid of them. We are engaged in a war of
great ideologies. This is not just a casual argu-
ment against slightly different philosophies.
This is a war of light against darkness, freedom against slavery, Godliness against athe-
ism. No man flying a war plane, no man with
a defensive gun in his hand, can possibly be
more important than the teacher.

WHAT, THEN — against this thirty years'
background — shall we do? In one of his
plays, *The Skin of Our Teeth,* Thorn-
ton Wilder writes: "Every good thing in
the world stands on the razor-edge of
danger." It has always been so with free
speech and will always remain so. Nothing
in the First Amendment to the Constitution promises that you can exercise free
speech without unpleasant consequences.
If you say something a senator or representative does not like, you may be exer-
cising a constitutional right, but he has
the privilege of getting behind Congressional immunity and throwing mud. We

must learn to accept such acts of cowardice as indicative of the character of those who employ them and come as near as we can to Benjamin Franklin's prescription. After he had been slandered by one of his fellow commissioners to France, he observed that when an adversary spattered you with mud the proper course was to let it dry — at which time it would easily brush off.

Senators and representatives have found new means of harassing private citizens, and some are ruthless in the employment of those techniques, so ruthless as to render their actions a clear and scandalous abuse of their legitimate powers. But the First Amendment offers no warranty, express or implied, that from time to time people will not send to Congress fools, knaves, bullies, self-seekers; the history of America shows that has happened even before our time. The only way to deal with such people is to make it politically unprofitable for them to employ their techniques.

Patrioteers can silence men by bullying them only so long as there are cowards abroad in the land. No senator or representative has power to stop anyone from saying anything; he is totally without authority to do so. He can stimulate the

timid to such fear that they abandon freedom. But if you are going to flee from
exercise of your rights when someone calls
you names, you are not worthy of freedom. Responsible thinkers do not yield to
pressure when the issue is drawn. You
may lose friends or comfort — Gandhi
and Nehru spent time in jail; Adenauer
was also put in jail. Freedom must be
won, not only on the battlefields, but at
the tea party, in the gossip column, at
every point where one life touches another — otherwise it is meaningless. You
cannot have freedom without risk.

For myself I do not believe that the
scholarly world is an association of Casper
Milquetoasts. It is true that the great emphasis upon tenure and upon security has
made the academic world hospitable to
some who like to have a shield between
them and the winds of doctrine, but education is no tender plant and is not easily
"controlled." Of all things the hardest to
control is thought.

The First Amendment assumes that
men want to speak their minds. It does
not proclaim a right to parrot somebody
else's mind. We know that when a person becomes a Communist he surrenders
the right to think for himself; he must

follow the party line. That has been demonstrated a countless number of times,
perhaps most dramatically when a "capi-
talist war of aggression" became a "war
of peace-loving democratic peoples" over-
night because Hitler turned on Stalin. The
First Amendment, I repeat, makes no
provision for a man to speak someone
else's mind; Charlie McCarthy has no
rights under the First Amendment, nor
has any other mouthpiece for the mind
of another.

There is something slightly absurd in
the claim that the right to "free speech"
is violated by questions regarding a man's
loyalty. Yet that is the claim which has
been made by men whose actions have
been so clandestine that few people knew
about them. It is absurd for a man to
claim his opinions are no one's business
when he is estopped from having any
opinions of his own by the nature of his
commitments to communist discipline.

It is possible to argue (though not with
much conviction since the courts have
spoken) that *no one* should be asked,
"Are you now or have you ever been a
Communist?" But, if it is proper, as the
courts say it is, to ask that question, it is
fantastic to assert that professors should

be exempt from responding. So long as
the question is not outlawed, there is no
basis for any claim to a "class" exemp-
tion. The question, the answer, and the
compulsion involved have none of them
anything whatever to do with "academic
freedom."

A positive approach to this problem is
to set freedom above security. Our generation is conterminous with an over-
accent upon social security, national security, security in appointments, security
in employment, old age security, and security in many other guises. If you con-
centrate your whole attention on security,
you cannot have your mind on freedom,
which is always risky. Benjamin Franklin said, "They that can give up essential
liberty to obtain a little temporary safety
deserve neither liberty nor safety." Therefore, a necessary step in recovering public
confidence is once again to set freedom
ahead of security.

Another constructive step is to reject
a current fallacy which plays directly into
the hands of those who menace liberty
in the name of protecting America. It is
the fallacy of supposing that the opposite
of something wrong must be something
right. A moment of analysis shows that

this is nonsense. It is based upon the assumption that opinion is distributed along a straight line. But that is not the nature of opinion, which scatters in all directions, to make a pattern which is infinitely complicated. This is so elementary that it seems hardly credible it can be doubted. Yet hundreds of thousands, if not millions, of our fellow-citizens have been gulled into the belief that, if a man proclaims himself an anti-Communist, those who oppose him must be in favor of communism.

If we express it diagrammatically, the point will be clear: the McCarthy diagram would be a straight line with communism at one end and McCarthy at the other; if you are not with McCarthy, you must be closer to communism. Change the diagram and you get nearer the truth: put communism in the center of a circle; put McCarthy, McCarran, Velde, Budenz, Bentley, and any others on the circumference; place yourself at your favorite place on the circumference. You may be right beside McCarthy and Company, or you may be 180 degrees away — yet you will be just as far from communism as he is, but still not close to him.

'There was a time when it was asserted

that the only choice was between communism and fascism, because democracy had too many weaknesses to survive. That was a manifestation of this same "either-or" fallacy. Today it takes the form of *either* communism *or* McCarthyism. The stupidity of this false alternative must be brought home: just as many kept their faith in democracy and wanted neither communism nor fascism, so you need not espouse either communism or McCarthyism. If you believe in freedom, help refute this nonsense that those who oppose un-American methods must be partisans of communism. You can hate both. That is the answer to people who say that because McCarthy, Jenner, Velde, and others are against communism they should not be criticized for abuses of Congressional immunity or assaults upon the integrity of honest men.

There are other means far better adapted to the desired ends. In politics, if the means are wrong, the ends will not be good. The classic instance of a fatal disparity between means and ends appears in one of the essays of Charles Lamb. He described how the Chinese first discovered the delicacy of roast pig — by the accidental burning of a house. Thereupon there was an epidemic of house-burning to roast other pigs. Men ultimately learned that there were more economical means of getting better roast pig. Some of our investigators have not yet learned this simple lesson; they are willing to burn the house of liberty to destroy invaders who have no more business being within it than a pig has inhabiting a human residence. Yet their pretense is that no other means are available, that the end justifies any measures, however drastic, however hurtful to liberty.

Here are the continuing obligations of students and teachers: neither cower nor invite martyrdom; seek no fight but avoid none when the issue is clear; be neither truculent nor pusillanimous. The pressures today are not nearly as great as those in times past. Security for communities, for industries, for profits, for occupations would bring only stagnation; it ultimately means the acceptance of controlled rigidity. There can be no liberty without hazard; freedom would be meaningless if it were safe.

Remember this: "Every good thing in the world stands on the razor-edge of danger."

CPSIA information can be obtained
at www.ICGtesting.com
Printed in the USA
LVHW081545231218
601532LV00018B/1380/P